A Book of Prayers from Around the World

Paix sur la Terre
FRENCH

世界和平
CHINESE

PEACE ON EARTH
ENGLISH

السلام في الأرض
ARABIC

Frieden auf Erden
GERMAN

Collected and Illustrated by Bijou Le Tord

A DOUBLEDAY BOOK FOR YOUNG READERS

A Doubleday Book for Young Readers
Published by
Delacorte Press
Bantam Doubleday Dell Publishing Group, Inc.
666 Fifth Avenue
New York, New York 10103
Doubleday and the portrayal of an anchor with a dolphin are trademarks of
Bantam Doubleday Dell Publishing Group, Inc.

Library of Congress Cataloging in Publication Data
Le Tord, Bijou,
Peace on earth; a book of prayers from around the world/Bijou Le Tord.
p.   cm.
Summary: A collection of prayers from around the world,
in such categories as "Children," "Animals," "The Sea," and "Songs and Celebrations."
ISBN 0-385-30692-X
1. Children — Prayer-books and devotions — English.   2. Prayers. [1. Prayers.] I.
Title.
BV4870.1.39 1992   291.4'5 — de20   91-39913   CIP   AC

Manufactured in the United States of America
October 1992
10 9 8 7 6 5 4 3 2 1

Grateful acknowledgment is made to the following for permission to print the copyrighted material listed below:

Bahá'í prayer, Bahá'u'lláh. Copyright 1954, © 1982, 1985, 1991 by the National Spiritual Assembly of the Bahá'ís of the United States.

"All You Creatures with Wings" and "The Voice of the Cricket" by Megan Boyd, © 1991 P.O. Box 27, Sag Harbor, N.Y. 11963. Original poems commissioned for *Peace on Earth.*

Untitled: Small prayer by Scott Chaskey, © 1991 P.O. Box 27, Sag Harbor, N.Y. 11963. Original poem commissioned for *Peace on Earth.*

The poem by V. Cokeham is from *Miracles: Poems by Children of the English-speaking World.* Edited by Richard Lewis and used with his permission. Originally published by Simon & Schuster, 1966. © Touchstone Center Publications, N.Y., 1989.

The lines from "i thank You God for most this amazing" are reprinted from *Complete Poems, 1913–1962,* e. e. cummings, by permission of Liveright Publishing Corporation. Copyright © 1923, 1925, 1931, 1935, 1938, 1939, 1940, 1944, 1945, 1946, 1947, 1948, 1949, 1950, 1951, 1952, 1953, 1954, 1955, 1956, 1957, 1958, 1959, 1960, 1961, 1962 by the trustees for the e. e. cummings Trust. Copyright © 1961, 1963, 1968 by Marion Morehouse Cummings.

"Light the Festive Candles" by Aileen Fisher, from *Skip Around the Year,* © 1967 by Aileen Fisher, used by permission of HarperCollins, N.Y.

"My People" from *The Dream Keeper and Other Stories* by Langston Hughes © 1962 by Alfred A. Knopf, N.Y.

"My paw is holy" by James Koller from *Songs of the Teton Sioux,* © 1976 James Koller, Black Sparrow Press, Santa Rosa, Calif.

Untitled poem from "Sea & Sky" from *33 Poems* by Robert Lax. © 1988 by Robert Lax and the Editor, Thomas Kellein. Used by permission of the author. Published by New Directions, N.Y.

"My Bath" by Madeleine L'Engle from *And God Bless Me* by Lee Bennett Hopkins, © 1982 by Alfred A. Knopf, N.Y.

"A Song for the Sunrise" from *Ceremony* by Leslie Marmon Silko. Copyright © 1977 by Leslie Marmon Silko. Used by permission of Viking Penguin, a division of Penguin Books USA, Inc., N.Y.

"Landscape with Yellow Birds" by Shuntarō Tanikawa from *The Selected Poems of Shuntarō Tanikawa,* translated by Harold Wright, © 1983 Farrar, Straus & Giroux, North Point Press, Berkeley, California.

Every effort has been made to locate all rights holders and to clear reprint permissions. If oversights have been made, we sincerely apologize and will be pleased to rectify the situation in future editions.

The following prayers and/or poems were adapted by Bijou Le Tord:

"Among the flowers I am moving reverently" / "Be gracious to me" / Canticle of the Sun / "How strong and good" / "Little angel of my God" / A little page's prayer / "Lord, the air smells good today" / "Lord, what a blessing is the sea" / Magic Prayer / "May all I say and all I think" / "My Lord, for the other clarity" (translation by Bijou Le Tord and Erika Wood) / "O Great Spirit whose voice" / "O Lord, Thou art in the little pebbles" / Silent Night / Song of Dzitbalche / "We bless you, cicada"

For my friend
Katie Howland

CONTENTS

And peace was a warming breeze
given by the sun.

—Peter Blue Cloud

Mattino e Sole

Morgen un Zon

Morning and Sun

Le Matin et le Soleil

Morgen und Sonne

I arise
        swift
as a raven's wing

I arise
        to meet the sun

Wa-wa.

I look away
from the dark
        of the night

I see dawn,
        now illuminating
the sky.

North America,
Iglulik Inuit People
Magic Prayer

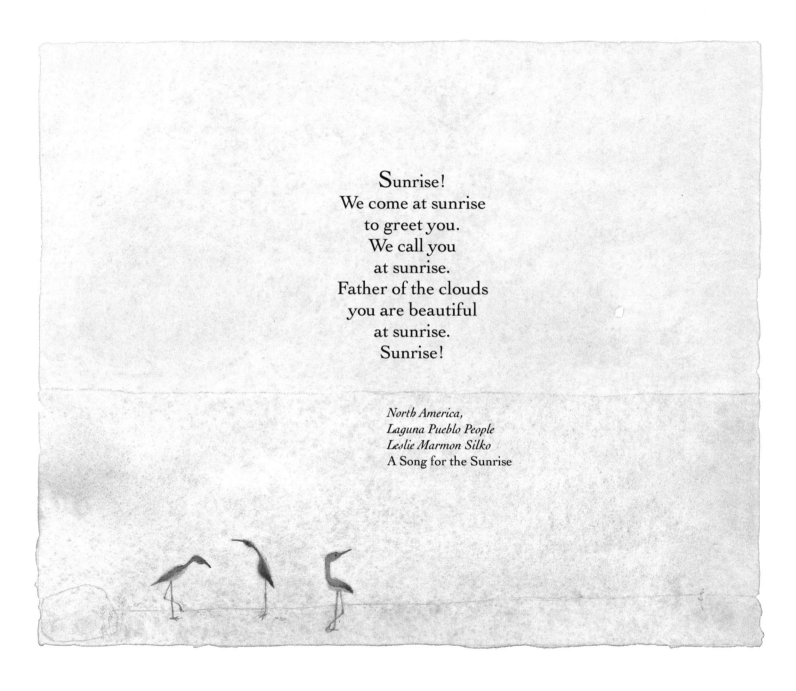

Sunrise!
We come at sunrise
to greet you.
We call you
at sunrise.
Father of the clouds
you are beautiful
at sunrise.
Sunrise!

North America,
Laguna Pueblo People
Leslie Marmon Silko
A Song for the Sunrise

Be praised, my Lord,
for all your creatures,
and first for brother sun,
who makes the day bright
        and luminous.

He is beautiful and radiant
        with great splendor,
he is the image of You,
        most high.

Be praised, my Lord,
for sister moon and the stars.
You placed them in the sky,
        so bright,
        and twinkling.

Be praised, my Lord,
for brother wind,
for the air and the clouds
and the airy skies
        and every kind of weather,
through which you give nourishment
        to all your
        creatures.

Be praised, my Lord,
　　for sister water,
who is very useful
　　and humble and precious
　　and pure.

Be praised, my Lord,
for brother fire
who illuminates the night,
　　he is beautiful and joyous
　　robust and strong.

Be praised, my Lord,
　　for our sister, mother earth,
who keeps us and watches us
and brings fruit and grain
　　of all kinds,
multicolored flowers,
　　and herbs.

Italy,
St. Francis of Assisi
Canticle of the Sun

God's bird in the morning
I'd be!
I'd set my heart
within a tree —
Close to His bed
and sing to Him,
Happily —
Happily,
a sunrise hymn.

England,
A little page's prayer

Dear Lord on high
Make a clear sky
Make the day fine
And let the sweet sun shine.

Holland,
Traditional

Plantas y Cosechas

पौधे और खेती

Plants and Harvesting

Pflanzen und Ernte

Les Plantes et la Recolte

Yellow flowers,
sweet flowers,

precious vanilla flowers
the crow's dark magic flowers

weave themselves together.

They are your
flowers, God.

We only borrow them:
your flowered drum,
your bells,
your song:

they are your flowers,
God.

Mexico,
The Refined Poet-King of
Nezahualcoyotl

1
Among the flowers I am moving reverently.

2
Among the flowers I am singing, dancing.

3
Berries ripen,
Fruit ripens.

North America,
Seneca People

Lord, the air smells good today,
straight from the mysteries
within
the garden
of God.

The trees in their prayer,
the birds in praise,
the first blue violets,
kneeling.

India,
Rumi

May all I say and all I think
     be in harmony with thee,
God within me,
        God beyond me,
maker of the trees.

North America,
Chinook People

How strong and good
　　and sure your earth smells,
　　and everything that grows there.

Bless us, our land,
　　and our people.

Bless our forests with mahogany,
　　wawa and cacao.

Bless our fields
　　with cassava and peanuts.

Be with us in our countries
　　and in all of Africa,
And in the whole world.

Africa,
Ashanti People

Dear Father, thank you
for the trees that give
us fruit, and the plants
that grow underground,
like peanuts. Amen.

Africa,
Rupesh N. Daya, age 7
A Prayer for Africa

It's harvest time,
It's harvest time,
How rich is nature's yield
In fruit of earth
And bush and tree,
From orchard, farm and field.

It's autumn time,
It's autumn time,
When leaves turn gold and red.
In smiling sky
And land and sea
God's glories are outspread.

It's Sukos time,
It's Sukos time,

This day of our Thanksgiving.
We hymn the praise
Of God above
For all the joys of living.

Israel,
Ilos Orleans
Sukos Song

1
For the Lord your God
is bringing you
into a good land,

2
a land of wheat
and barley,
of vines
and fig trees
and pomegranates,

3
a land
of olive trees
and honey,

4
a land
where
you may eat
bread
to your fill.

5
Praise Him!

Deuteronomy 8:7–11

Thank you for the apples like berries
that color the trees and the sky.

I want to leap and talk
and then sleep in the air

where your fruits ripen and dance.
Mother of earth, this is my prayer!

Oh, yes—at night
when we turn from father light,

please cover my cloud bed
with your phosphorescence.
Thank you for your apples.

North America,
Scott Chaskey
Small prayer

дéти

RUSSIAN

Bambini

ITALIAN

Children

ENGLISH

こども

JAPANESE

Niños

SPANISH

O Great Spirit
whose voice I hear
in the winds,

and whose breath
gives life to all
the world,

Hear me!
I am small
and weak,
I need your strength
and wisdom.

Make me wise
so that I may know
the things
you have
taught
my people.

Let me learn
the lessons you have
hidden in
every leaf
and rock.

North America,
Native American People

I love you
my God!
I love you
more
than anything
in the world!

Praise to you, God!

Russia,
Traditional

there are birds
so there is sky
there is sky
so there are balloons
there are balloons
so children are running
children are running
so there is laughter
there is laughter
so there is sadness
so there is prayer
and ground for kneeling
there is ground
so water is flowing
and there's today and tomorrow
there is a yellow bird
so with all colors forms and movements
there is the world

Japan,
Shuntarō Tanikawa
Landscape with Yellow Birds

God
make my life
a little light
within the world
to glow;
A little
flame
to burn
bright,
wherever
I may
go.

England,
Traditional

O Lord
Let my spirit
   glow
    so brightly,

that darkness
will disappear.

Pakistan,
Islamic
A child's prayer

Two little eyes to look to God;
Two little ears to hear his word;
Two little feet to walk his ways;
Two little lips to sing his praise;
Two little hands to do his will
And one little heart to love him still.

Wales,
Traditional

Little
angel of
my God,
be always
near me,
when I play
and when
I work.

Always,
always be
with me.

Italy,
Traditional

There is an umbrella
In the sky,
It must be raining
In Heaven
I have one prayer to say to God
Don't let it rain tomorrow.

England,
V. Cokeham, age 10

Farmer St. Isidore,
Take away the rain
And bring the sun out
Once again.

Ecuador,
Children's prayer to stop rain

La Mer

सागर

The Sea

El Mar

Bahati

O Lord,

Thou art in the little pebbles
As well as in the calm open sea;

I bow to Thee.

India,
"Sukla Yajur," Veda XVI

Dear God, be good to me.
The sea is so wide,
And my boat is so small.

France,
Breton fisherman's prayer

Lord,
   what a blessing
        is the sea
     with fish
       in plenty

Ghana,
A fisherman's prayer

Be gracious
to me,
my Father,
hold up
my
boat.

South America,
Andean Yahgan People

My bath is the ocean
and I am a continent
with hills and valleys
and earthquakes and storms.
I put the two mountain peaks of my knees
under water and bring them up again.

Our earth was like that—
great churnings and splashings,
and continents appearing and disappearing.

Only you, O God, know about it all,
and understand, and take care
of all your creation.

North America,
Madeleine L'Engle
My Bath

Little drops of water,
little grains of sand,
make the mighty ocean,
and the pleasant land.

Little deeds of kindness,
little words of love,
Help to make earth happy,
like the heaven above.

England,
Traditional

Animales

ζῷα

Animals

どうぶつ

Zwierzęta

You are singing, little dove,
on the branches of the silk-cotton tree.

And there is also the cuckoo,
And many other little birds.

All are rejoicing,
the songbirds of our god, our Lord.

At daybreak all is jubilant.

Let only joy, only songs,
be in our minds!

Mexico,
Song of Dzitbalche

All you creatures with wings,
     Eagle and Bee,
          Ichneumon Fly and Wren,

as you fly on
     our Mother's breath,

I, your little sister,
     ask you,

carry my heartbeat morning prayer
          in your wingbeat:

"How I love you—
 How I thank you—"

Carry it up to our Mother's lap,
   carry it into our Father's ear,

     carry it
          three times around
               the belly of Earth.

North America,
Megan Boyd
All You Creatures with Wings

Glory be to God for dappled things—
     For skies of couple-colour as a brinded cow;
          For rose-moles all in stipple upon trout that swim;
Fresh-firecoal chestnut-falls; finches' wings;
     Landscape plotted and pieced—fold, fallow, and plough;
          And all trades, their gear and tackle and trim.

All things counter, original, spare, strange;
     Whatever is fickle, freckled (who knows how?)
          With swift, slow; sweet, sour; adazzle, dim;
He fathers-forth whose beauty is past change.
                              Praise him.

England,
Gerard Manley Hopkins
Pied Beauty

We
bless you,
cicada,

high in the trees.

You sip
a dew drop
and whistle
like a king.

What you see
is yours:
all the soft
meadows
and furry
mountains.

Yet you do no harm
in the farmer's field.

We
bless you,
cicada.

Greece,
Anonymous

Dear Father,
hear and bless
Thy beasts and singing birds,

And guard
with tenderness
Small things that have no words.

England,
Traditional

Flying out from
the Great Buddha's nose:
a swallow.

Japan,
Issa
A Haiku

Puppies
and kittens,
O Lord
I pray for them
to grow
bigger than
they are now.

North America,
Bijou Le Tord

The bee,
climbing the last blossom,
hears.
"I never forget you,
oh, forever last one."

I am hearing.
I, in my place, am hearing
your voice, dear Father,
the honeybee song
deep in the field.

Lift me to your listening place.
I am singing my own small prayer
among the voices of the field.
I am the voice
like the cricket.
Bring me close to you
so you can hear my voice
inside all the voices.

Is your listening deep in
Earth's belly?
I will put my ear down
and I will listen.
Now I put my voice
on the cricket's wings
and send him down
the earthways to you.

Are you in Earth's heart?
When my heart hurts, hear
my heart's voice, God,
calling you under her stones.
When I am scared in the dark
hear my heartbeat
in the night rain.

You listen with the doe's ears
as she stands still
in the footprints of her listening:
hear me, dear Father.

And when I hear
that you are listening
I will rise up tall inside myself
the way the cricket hears
his own sound strong
inside his black shell
as the voice of the mountain.

North America,
Megan Boyd
The Voice of the Cricket

My paw is holy
herbs are everywhere
my paw
herbs are everywhere

My paw is holy
everything is holy
my paw
everything is holy

North America,
adapted by
James Koller
From Songs of the Teton Sioux

赞美和感谢

Praises and Thanks

Lodi e Grazie

Alabanza y Gracias

תהילות ותשבחות

i thank You God for most this amazing
day:for the leaping greenly spirits of trees
and a blue true dream of sky;and for everything
which is natural which is infinite which is yes

North America,
e.e. cummings

1 · *And it came to pass, that, as*
he was praying in a certain place,
when he ceased, one of his disciples
said unto him, Lord teach us to pray,
as John also taught his disciples.
2 · *And he said unto them, When*
ye pray, say:

Luke 11 : 1–2

9 · Our Father which art in heaven,
Hallowed be thy name.
10 · Thy kingdom come. Thy
will be done in earth, as *it is*
in heaven.
11 · Give us this day our daily bread.
12 · And forgive us our debts,
as we forgive our debtors.
13 · And lead us not into temptation,
but deliver us from evil: For thine
is the kingdom, and the power,
and the glory, for ever. Amen.

Matthew 6:9–13
King James Version

Blessed art Thou
O Lord our God
King of the world
who makes the fruit
of the tree.

Blessed art Thou
O Lord our God
King of the world
whose word makes all
things on the earth.

Blessed art Thou
O Lord our God
King of the world
who brings food
out of the earth.

Blessed art Thou
O Lord our God
King of the world
who gives clothes
to cover our bodies.

Blessed art Thou
O Lord our God
King of the world
who makes sweet smelling
wood and plants.

Blessed art Thou
O Lord our God
King of the world
who has kept us alive
until now so we may
find joy in what has
just come to us.

Blessed art Thou
O Lord our God
King of the world
who has created
the wonderful things of
earth and heaven.

North America,
Hebrew prayer
for little ones

أغنياء واحتفالات

Lieder und Feiern

Songs and Celebrations

Canciones y Celebraciones

歌曲和庆典

Light the first of eight tonight—
the farthest candle to the right.

Light the first and second, too,
when tomorrow's day is through.

Then light three, and then light four—
every dusk one candle more

Till all eight burn bright and high,
honoring a day gone by

When the Temple was restored,
rescued from the Syrian lord,

And an eight-day feast proclaimed—
The Festival of Lights—well named

To celebrate the joyous day
when we regained the right to pray
to our one God in our own way.

North America,
Aileen Fisher
Light the Festive Candles
(For Hanukkah)

O sing unto the Lord
a new song:
sing unto the Lord,
all the earth.

Psalm 96:1–4

the
dove

the
dove

the
dove

the
dove

comes
down

comes
down

&
breaks

the
air

North America,
Robert Lax
From Sea & Sky

Blessed is the spot, and the house,
and the place, and the city,

and the heart, and the mountain,
and the refuge, and the cave,
and the valley, and the land,

and the sea, and the island,
and the meadow where mention
of God hath been made,

and His praise glorified.

Iran,
Bahá'u'lláh
Bahá'í prayer

Silent night,
   holy night.

All is calm,
   all is bright

Round yon Virgin
   Mother and Child.

Holy infant,
   so tender and
   mild,

Sleep in heavenly peace.

Sleep in heavenly peace.

Austrian,
Joseph Morh
Silent Night

Señora doña María,
I come from far away
And I bring a pair of rabbits
To the little Child today.

Squash, I bring, potatoes,
And flour for poor Ana.
Mamma, Pappa send regards;
So does old Aunt Juana.

In the crèche of Bethlehem
Are sun, moon, stars galore,
The Virgin and St. Joseph
And Jesus in the straw.

Chile,
Traditional

'Tis a gift to be simple,
'Tis a gift to be free;
'Tis a gift to come down
    where we ought to be.
And when we find ourselves in the place
    just right,
'Twill be in the valley
    of love and delight.

When true simplicity is gained,
To bow and to bend
    We will not be ashamed.
To turn, turn
    will be our delight,
Till by turning, turning
    we come round right.

North America,
Shaker song
Simple Gifts

Noche y Luna

ночь и луна́

Night and Moon

रात और चाँद

夜和月亮

the sun
she
is setting
in the tall grass
beneath the pines

where the heart
beats
one with the land

where the mule deer
approach
their antlers raised

where with palms
upturned
we pray

North America,
Charlie Mehrhoff

The night is beautiful,
So the faces of my people.

The stars are beautiful,
So the eyes of my people.

Beautiful, also, is the sun.
Beautiful, also, are the souls of my people.

North America,
Langston Hughes
My People

We are the stars which sing
We sing with our light.
We are the birds of fire
We fly across the heaven,
Our light is a star.
We make a road for Spirits,
A road for the Great Spirit.

North America,
Algonkian People

My bed has four little corners,
Four little angels who keep me company,

Two at my feet, two at my head.
The Virgin Mary is my companion,
who says to me, "Lupita, sleep and rest.

Don't be afraid of anything."

Mexico,
Traditional

I see the moon,
    And the moon sees me;
God bless the moon,
    And God bless me.

England,
Traditional

My Lord, for the other clarity
that you have given my soul

                              I thank you

My Lord, for the tranquility
that you have given my soul

                              I thank you

My Lord, night has come
You close my eyes before the day
And me, I'll paint once again
Paintings for you
On the earth and in the sky

Russia,
Marc Chagall

Now I lay me down to sleep,
   I pray Thee, Lord, Thy child to keep;
Thy love go with me all the night,

and wake me with the morning light.

England,
Traditional

Index of Titles

Index of Authors

Index of First Lines

I would like to thank:
George Nicholson, Vice President and Publisher at Delacorte,
for his great support;
Mary Cash, Senior Editor,
whose intelligent and reassuring comments helped me along; and
Lynn Braswell, Art Director,
for her exquisite sense of color.
Thanks and warm wishes
to the people and friends at home and around the world
who offered their generous help for the project:
Fran Silverblank, Megan Boyd, Scott Chaskey, Erika Wood,
Norah and Canio Pavone, Robert Lax, Peter Blue Cloud,
Brother Benet Tvedten, O.S.B., Justa Wawira, Philo Ikonya,
Sam Mburne, Kerstin Backman, Deborah H. Christensen, Teresa Rijks,
Isabel Randall, Gloria E. Hatrick, K. Nielsen, Urmila Varma,
Margot Dalingwater, Paul Ewen, Katherine Hoffman,
Donia Clenman, Patti Farmer, Henriette Major, Jose Patterson,
Hilda Adiambo, Nancy Bohac Flood, Stella Barnes,
Elaine Glover-Cyangabo, Ruby E. McCreight, Teri Welles,
Alison Lohans, and my sister Yannick Le Tord.

This book is set in 14-point Cochin
The illustrations are done in Windsor Newton
watercolors on Arches 140-pound cold press watercolor paper
Typography by Lynn Braswell

HIGHGROVE